AQS Publishing

Heirloom Quilted Nursery

Florence Riesen

Located in Paducah, Kentucky, the American Quilter's Society (AQS) is dedicated to promoting the accomplishments of today's quilters. Through its publications and events, AQS strives to honor today's quiltmakers and their work and to inspire future creativity and innovation in quiltmaking.

American Quilter's Society
P. O. Box 3290 • Paducah, KY 42002-3290
www.AmericanQuilter.com

Additional copies of this book may be ordered from the American Quilter's Society, PO Box 3290, Paducah, KY 42002-3290, or online at www.AmericanQuilter.com.

Text © 2009, Author, Florence Riesen
Artwork © 2009 American Quilter's Society

Executive Editor: Andi Milam Reynolds
Editor: Linda Baxter Lasco
Graphic Design: Lynda Smith
Cover Design: Michael Buckingham
Photography: Charles R. Lynch
Some photos shot on location at Babies in Bloom, Paducah, Kentucky.

Library of Congress Cataloging-in-Publication Data

Riesen, Florence.
  Heirloom quilted nursery / by Florence Riesen.
    p. cm.
  ISBN 978-1-57432-984-1
  1. Quilting--Patterns. 2. Nurseries. 3. Interior decoration. I. Title.
  TT835.R537 2009
  746.46'041--dc22

                          2009000918

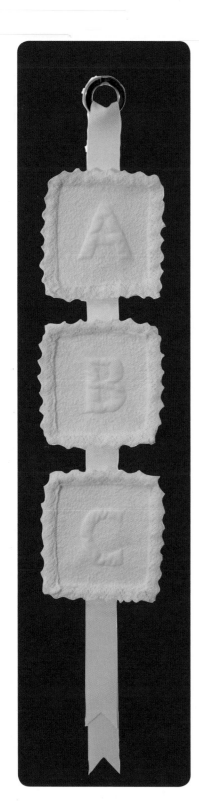

Dedication

To my husband, Richard, and our son, Peter, whose response to my meager attempts is always enthusiastic and encouraging.

Acknowledgments

Thank you to Diane Gaudynski for the inspiration of her innovative quilting and for the photograph of the family bib in her book *Guide to Machine Quilting*, which, as I think about it, was probably what got me going on this project.

Everyone needs a couple of quilting friends like mine. Thanks to Didi Fuller, who has an excellent eye for color and an enormous stash of fabric she is willing to share at any time, and to Bev Underwood, who brings melt-in-your-mouth baked ham slices and extravagant desserts to our quilting get-togethers and lets me take her quilt classes when she can't make it.

Thank you to AQS for taking on this different kind of project. To Linda Baxter Lasco, senior editor; Michael Buckingham, cover designer; Lynda Smith, graphic designer; and Charles R. Lynch, photographer, my heartfelt thanks.

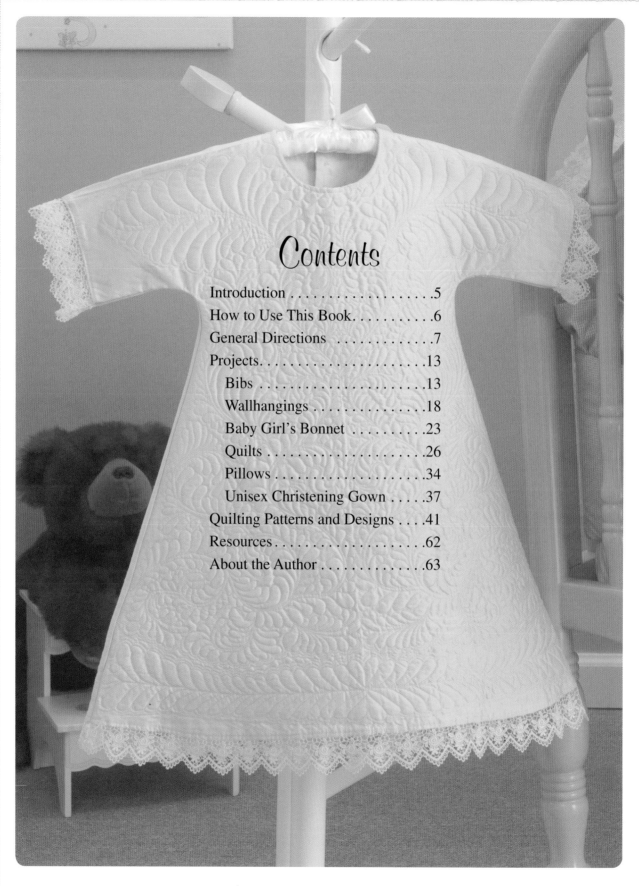

Contents

Introduction

This book is for all women who know and love someone who is expecting a baby and would like to make an elegant, heirloom gift for the mother-to-be. Sharing the joy and anticipation of a friend or relative's new baby is a delightful experience. Like many of you, I began receiving invitations to baby showers in my early twenties and, as I recall, was going to showers with my mother even earlier than that. I am now retired and still going to baby showers. What, though, to give?

It is nice to give a special gift. Disposable diapers are needed but I would much rather give something unusual, memorable perhaps, rather than useful—a one-of-kind gift, something I've made. It's not always possible, of course. Sometimes even making a baby quilt took more time than I had, especially during the years when I was working. So while many of us have been making lovely baby quilts for years, with whimsical designs, in primary colors and pastels, we may be looking for something different.

When looking through Diane Gaudynski's *Guide to Machine Quilting*, I saw that the dedication page featured a bib made by her great-great-grandmother. It was a machine-quilted bib. I had been invited to a niece's shower and decided to try making one like it. I went to shops looking for bibs and found many sizes and shapes, all very functional, many of them made of terry cloth or plastic, but nothing fancy or exceptional. So the first step was to design and make the bib itself. I drew some bib patterns and began drawing quilting designs.

Over the next couple of months I made three bibs, all different, gave them away at three different showers, and saw how enthusiastically they were received. The expectant mothers wanted to frame them and hang them on the wall. I could have taken many orders for bibs, but not wanting to spend so much of my time sewing bibs, I decided to put together the directions so anyone with some sewing and quilting experience could make one. Thus the idea for this book. I sent some bib samples to the American Quilter's Society. They liked them but wanted to see some additional items, so I added other ideas, keeping in mind the importance of the heirloom and elegant look for all the projects.

The bibs especially, and most of the other projects, are not meant to be functional by any means. I doubt if any baby would wear an heirloom bib except for a photo. They are meant for mothers who want something lovely of heirloom quality to show and eventually put away with all the baby mementoes. The unisex christening gown is also meant for use at special religious occasions or for photographs.

So this is a new idea for traditional heirloom-style handmade gifts. Some of the smaller projects can be completed in one or two days, depending on how many interruptions you have and how much quilting you add.

How to Use This Book

Customizing Your Project

There are a number of choices you can make in putting together your individual project. You may mix, match, enlarge, or reduce the designs to create new combinations. You could take the walking bear, for example, reduce the size to 2"–3" to fit the center of a bib, or increase the size to 15"–18" to fit the center of a quilt.

Another option is to eliminate the inner row of feathers in one of the heart designs to make room for a child's name or initials. Hopefully you will be inspired to think of ways to create your own personal work of art. I have used more traditional designs for the centers, but you could quilt in a race car, a soccer ball, or Cabbage Patch-looking doll.

You will sometimes need to refer to the section with general directions when making your project. Techniques specific to an individual project are included with that project. Techniques common to all the projects are found in the general directions.

Level of Experience

Intermediate or advanced sewing and quilting experience is necessary, including knowing how to sew on a binding, and some experience with free-motion quilting.

The book does not give detailed directions on free-motion quilting, so I have listed several books as references for background quilting ideas (see Resources, page 62). If you can follow a design line with free-motion quilting you should be able to complete a project. If you are able to add background embellishments, that will make your project all the more lovely. Otherwise you can just leave the background without quilting, or add grid lines with the June Tailor® Grid Marker™ ruler, and then quilt them with a walking foot.

Care of an Heirloom Project

After your heirloom project has been hanging in baby's room for a year or more, the recipient may want to clean it and put it away.

Heirloom projects can be carefully hand-washed in cold water, much the same way you would wash a fine wool sweater, and flattened out to dry without changing the look too much. If you put these projects into the dryer, even without heat, they will shrink up and get a crinkled look, but you may want that effect.

Look at the ELISE (page 32) quilt and you will see that it is crinkled more than the others in the book. That is because I wanted to see how it would look after five minutes in the dryer on cool air only. Perhaps it is even more antique looking than the others.

General Directions

Supplies

Basic sewing supplies

Basic quilting supplies

Free-motion foot

Walking foot

Blue water-soluble marker (thick)

Wash-A-Way® water-soluble thread

60-weight cotton thread for the bobbin

Silk thread for the top

Microtex Sharp needles, size 70/10

Wool or cotton batting

Poly batting for trapunto

June Tailor® Grid Marker™ ruler

Light box

Chopstick or crochet hook

Lace (amount varies for each project)

Buttons (when needed)

    choose ones that add to the heirloom look

Loop and ribbon for wallhanging

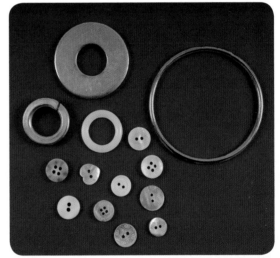

Fabric and Batting

Egyptian cotton, cotton sateen, Kona cotton, and dupioni shantung silk fabric all work up nicely. Washable cotton fabric is a good choice for a baby quilt that is going to be used, while silk is the choice for a project that will be decorative only, such as a wallhanging. Silk projects have a softer feel to them than cotton ones, but most heirloom projects are going to be displayed rather than used, so the feel is not so important. I prefer white or off-white, to give the heirloom look. Pale pink or blue may be used as well.

I do not prewash my fabric for heirloom projects, but if you have cotton fabric in your stash that is prewashed, it will be fine. Do not prewash silk fabric. When your project is finished you will spray or dip in a rinse of cold water both cotton and silk fabric to take out the blue markings and wash-a-way stabilizing stitches. Blot dry with a towel and lay out to dry.

I primarily use wool batting. On some of the samples I added some poly trapunto over cotton batting to see how much difference it would make. I think it does add a little more puff to the design, but not significantly, so I have gone back to wool batting only. You will achieve a very nice puff with wool batting and it saves having to cut away that extra layer of poly batting. The trapunto technique may be used in any of the designs you choose.

Lettering

If you choose to put baby's name on your project, you will need lettering. Simple fonts show up better in quilting than complicated ones because the little squiggles often get covered up in the background quilting. If you have a monogram with curlicues, tendrils, and swirls, enlarge it enough so that stippling in the background will make the small parts in the letters stand out.

I have included three alphabet samples that may be enlarged or reduced to fit your project (pages 42–44).

Techniques

Techniques individual to each project are specifically written out with those projects. Techniques common to all the projects are found here.

Seam Allowance

All seam allowances are ¼" unless otherwise noted.

Marking Quilting Designs

Find the center of your project by making vertical and horizontal lines through the center of your fabric with a blue water-soluble marker

(photo 1). (Most of the patterns have the center point marked for you.)

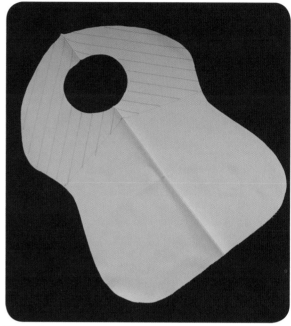

Photo 1

Choose a quilting border first and, with the help of a light box, mark it onto the fabric with a water-soluble blue marker. Mark the center design after the border is drawn so you can be sure it will be centered properly within the borders.

If the center design is not symmetrical, place it within the border so it looks balanced vertically and horizontally. If you make a mistake, spray with plain water to remove the marks, wait until dry, and try again.

Trapunto

Wool batting alone will give a nice trapunto look to your project, so it is not necessary to add trapunto. However, if you want to emphasize the design a little more, layer a poly batting on the back of the areas with quilting designs and pin in place. Using a free-motion foot, sew around the edges of your quilting design with wash-a-way thread in both the top and bobbin. (Be sure to remove this thread from your machine when you are finished!)

Carefully trim away the poly batting beyond the stitching lines around the designs. Then sandwich your project for quilting.

Sandwiching Your Project for Quilting

If the project (like a quilt or pillow top) will be trimmed and bound, place the backing fabric (same size as the front) right side down on a table or other flat surface. Smooth it out and tape it in place.

Lay the batting on top of the backing, and lay the top (right side up) on the batting (photo 2).

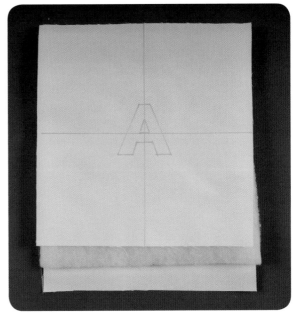

Photo 2

Align the edges and add stabilizing stitching or pin the layers together with #1 safety pins (photo 3).

If the project (like a bib) will be sewn and turned, place the batting on a table or other flat surface and lay the project back and top, right sides together, on the batting. Pin around the edges with straight pins.

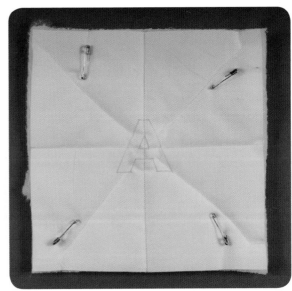

Photo 3

Sew around the edges, leaving an opening for turning. Turn right side out and proceed with the stabilizing stitching and quilting.

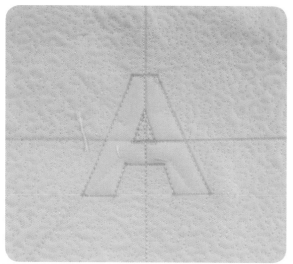

Photo 4

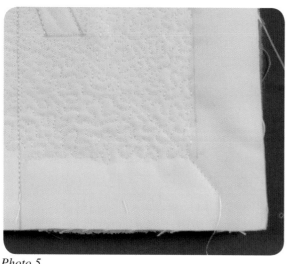

Photo 5

Add Stabilizing Stitching

Add stabilizing stitches with washaway thread along the length of the spine of any feather designs and any other place you want held in place while you quilt. I recommend lots of wash-a-way stitching before you begin to quilt. It washes out, so it won't show on the finished project.

When you are stitching, always use both hands to manipulate the fabric to keep the layers together and flat so the foot won't push a bubble of fabric ahead of the needle and form a wrinkle. Be sure to remove the wash-a-way thread from your machine when you are finished.

Quilting the Design

Put cotton thread in the bobbin and silk thread in the top and check the tension. All quilting is done with this combination of threads.

Begin quilting at or near the center and work out toward the edges. Optionally, sew once again around a center design about ⅛" away from the first stitching to give a finished looked to the design (photo 4).

For curved lines, use a free-motion foot with the feed dogs lowered.

For straight lines, use a walking foot with the feed dogs raised.

Most projects have extra fabric around the edges, so you have the option of adding background quilting all the way to the edges or trimming off more fabric up closer to the border pattern (photo 5).

Squaring Up the Project

Square up the straight-edge project with a square ruler. Most of the projects have extra fabric at the edges for you to work with when you square up.

Preparing the Edges

Smooth out the sandwiched layers to the trimmed edges and pin the three layers together with straight pins. With a walking foot, sew the edges together (photo 6).

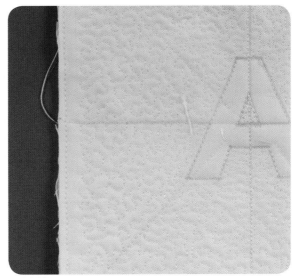

Photo 6

Adding Lace Trim

On the front of the project, start sewing at a corner and make a small tuck in the lace. Continue sewing around the project ¼" from the edge, with the decorative lace edge facing in toward the center of the project. In other words, the right (front) side of the lace is against the right side of the project (photo 7). Do not stretch the lace. Be generous with the lace as you lay it down to sew.

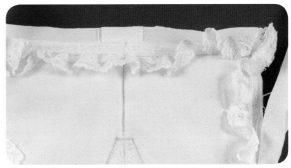

Photo 7

At each corner, put in three small tucks—one just before the corner, one at the corner, and one just beyond the corner. When you complete the perimeter and are back at the beginning corner, put in the last two tucks and leave enough lace to sew the end to the beginning edge by hand, concealing the connection. Trim and hand finish (photo 8).

Adding Binding

Sew the 2¼" binding strips together with bias (45-degree angle) seams. Trim the seam allowances. Fold the binding in half lengthwise and

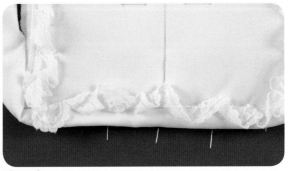

Photo 8

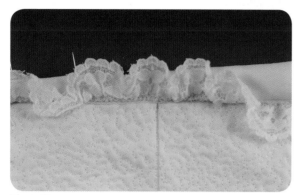

Photo 9

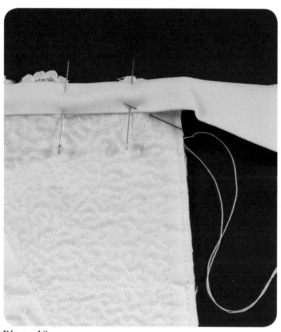

Photo 10

press with a hot iron so that you have one long continuous binding to work with. Align the raw edges and sew the binding to the outside edge of the top of the project, ¼" in from the edge and on top of the sewing line you used for adding the lace trim.

Turning the Lace Trim

After applying the binding but before you hand sew it in place, flatten back the lace away from the project. Sew along the top of the lace through all layers (lace, binding, and project) just at the edge of the lace, to make it face to the outside of the project (photo 9). This is impossible to do at the corners, so sew just up to the corner and stop there. The corner will have a little fullness because of the tucks you put in the lace and will lie flat.

Hand Finishing the Binding

Hand sew the binding to the back of the project (photo 10).

Removing Basting and Markings

With a water spray bottle, spritz out all the wash-a-way thread basting and blue water-soluble markings. You may rinse under cold water if you prefer. Blot with a towel and flatten out to dry.

Pattern CD

All the patterns and quilting designs are on the CD-ROM included with this book. They can be printed on standard 8½" x 11" paper. Designs larger than one page will print with registration marks so pages can be accurately overlapped and taped in place. See the ReadMe file for further instructions.

Bibs

Vander

Eli

Peter

William

Ethan

Luc

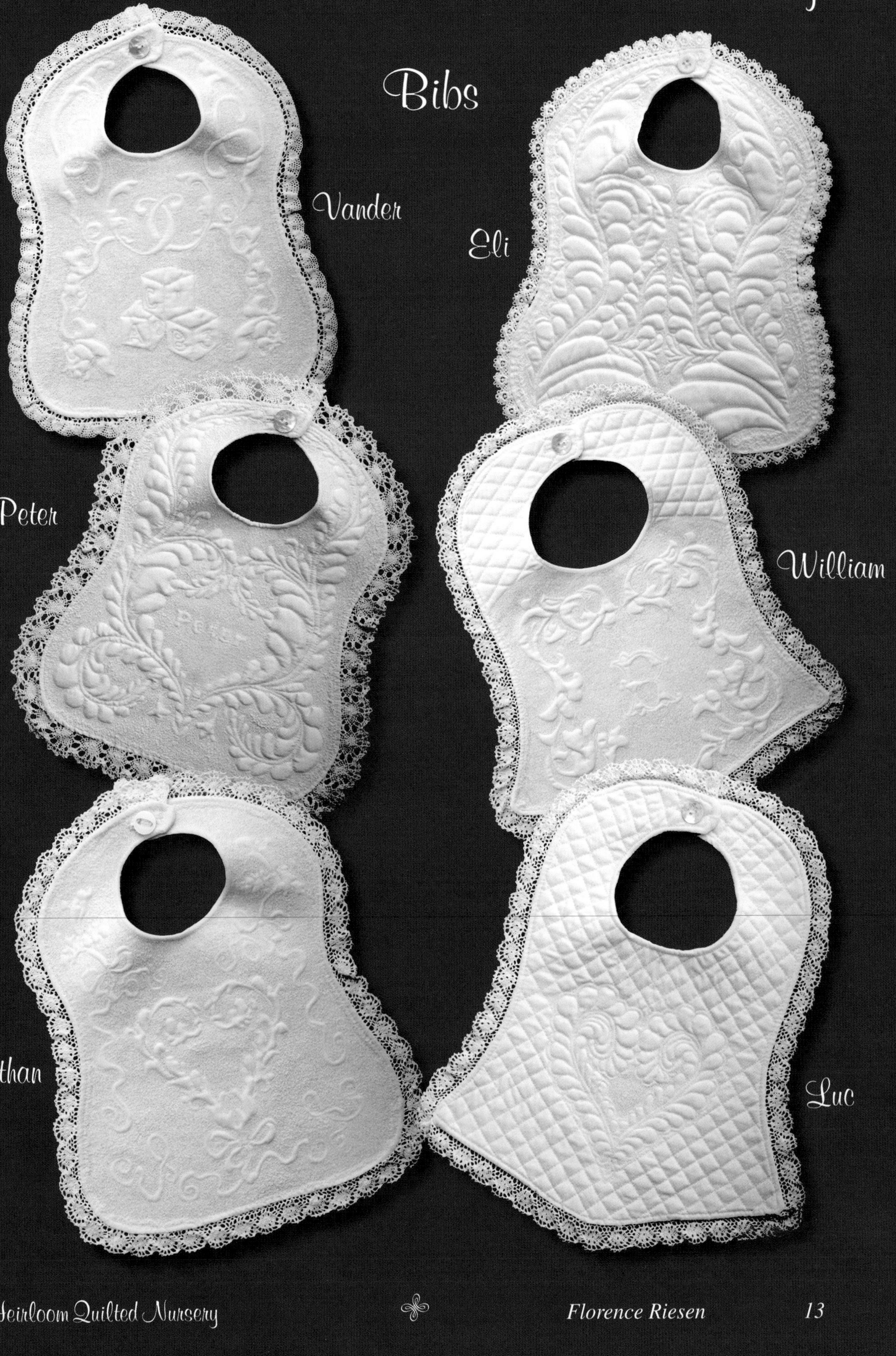

Bibs

Patterns

Bib 1 Large size with angled corners

Bib 2 Medium size with rounded corners

Bib 3 Small size with straight edges

Materials

Fabric: ½ yard

Lace: 1¼ yards

Batting: ½ yard

Button

Photo 1

Photo 2

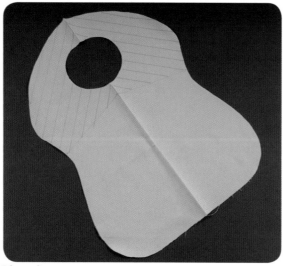

Photo 3

Cutting

Print a copy of the pattern you have chosen, using paper heavy enough to trace around.

Fold your fabric selvage-to-selvage, then fold the fabric again, the width of the bib pattern, so that you have 4 layers of fabric.

Place the half-pattern on the double-folded edge of the fabric (opposite the selvages) aligning the fold line of the pattern with the fold of the fabric. Draw around it with a pencil or blue water-soluble marker (photo 1).

Remove the pattern and pin through all 4 layers inside the drawn line.

Cut on the drawn line (photo 2). You are cutting out the front and back of the bib at the same time.

Cut out wool batting the same size as the bib.

Mark the quilting design on the right side of the bib front (photo 3).

Sewing the Lace

Beginning at the top, roll over the end of the lace twice to hide the raw edge of the lace. With the rolled side up, pin the roll ¼" from the center fold of the bib. Pin the lace around the bib at 1" intervals, making sure the lace isn't stretched (photo 4). You will need to be generous with the amount of lace so it will not buckle under the edge of the bib when you finish.

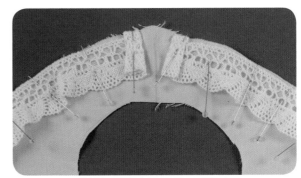
Photo 4

At the bottom corners put 3 tucks in the lace—one before the corner, one at the corner, and one just beyond the corner (photo 5). Cut the lace about ½" beyond the ending point and roll over the end as before, pinning ¼" in from the center fold.

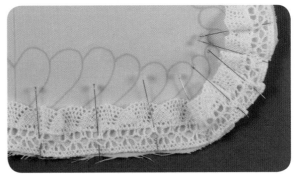
Photo 5

Using a walking foot sew on the lace around the entire bib with a ¼" seam allowance.

Joining the Bib Layers

Sandwich the layers with the batting on the bottom, then the bib back right side up, and the bib front right side down (photo 6). At the top of the neck where you will later put the button and buttonhole, cut through to the center of the neck along the fold line, making sure you are not cutting the lace trim. Feel the lace with your fingers and push it back. Carefully align the edges of the 3 layers and pin them all the way around including around the neck, which still has the wool batting inside to stabilize it.

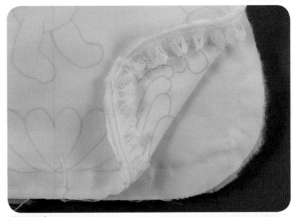
Photo 6

Begin sewing at the bottom of the bib with a walking foot, starting about 2" in from the left side (photo 7). Continue sewing, exactly on top of the stitching line of the lace. When you come to the top, continue to within ¼" of the end of

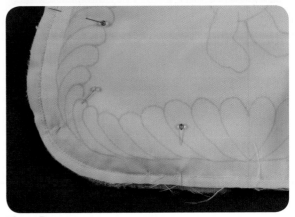
Photo 7

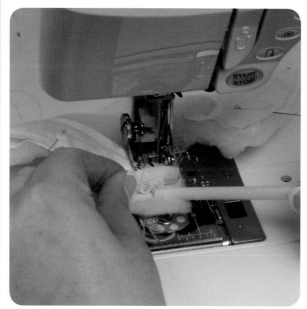

Photo 8

Photo 9

the center cut. Stop, pivot, and with a stiletto push back the lace, away from the ¼" seam allowance, so it doesn't get caught in the seam.

Continue sewing around the neck, a scant ¼" away from the edge at the neck only. Keeping the correct seam allowance in the inside neck area will require almost constant adjustment of the fabric as you are sewing because it is a small curve and you don't have the previous sewing line from the lace to follow. So sew slowly around the neck. As you come up on the top edge again, you will need to stop and push back the lace with a stiletto, away from the ¼" seam allowance (photo 8). Again, you do not want to sew the lace into the seam! Finish sewing about 2"–3" from where you began, leaving an opening for turning.

Trim, Snip, and Turn

Cut away the batting from the neck and discard. Cut away any excess batting that may be sticking out on the sides of the bib.

If you used one of the patterns with an indented side, snip 4 times, ¼" apart, on each side (photo 9). You do not need to snip the neck area.

Pull the bib front and back apart, keeping the batting and the back together, and turn the bib right side out. Gently pull the lace out from the layers. When you reach the top, if the ends do not turn out all the way, insert a chopstick or a crochet hook and gently finish pushing them out. With your hands, flatten out the bib and make sure the lace hasn't been caught in the seam. If it has, you must correct that now.

Hand Finishing

Working from the back side, turn under the opening at the bottom of the bib, pin it in place, and hand sew this small section together (photo 10). Tack down the rolled-under lace ends by hand, on both sides of the neck opening, to hold them in place.

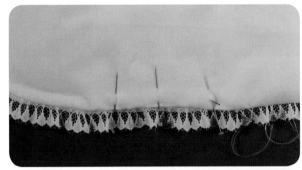
Photo 10

Topstitching

With silk thread in the top of your machine, cotton thread in the bobbin and using a walking foot, add topstitching around the edge of the bib ⅛" in from the edge. Start at the top of the neck and sew around the entire edge of the bib, including the inside of the neck. Flatten out the bib with your hands while you are carefully sewing this additional topstitch trim.

Quilting

Add stabilizing stitching (not shown) and quilt the design (photo 11).

Finishing Touches

On the top left side add a buttonhole. (On some of my bibs I accidentally worked from the wrong side of the bib and put the buttonhole on the right side. I was feeling badly about it until I remembered that men's and women's clothing are buttoned on opposite sides anyway.) Sew a button onto the top right side.

Rinse or spritz out any wash-a-way thread and blue markings. Let dry.

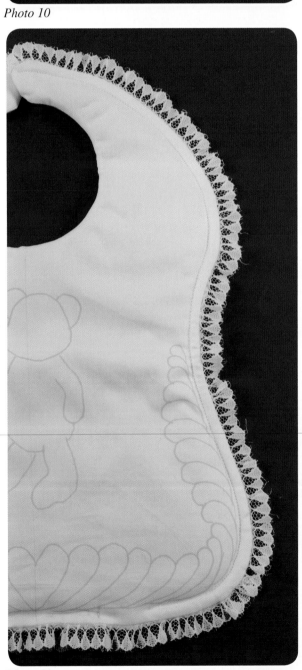
Photo 11

Wallhangings

In addition to the Cameo Bear and ABC wallhangings shown here, you can make other wallhangings using the border designs and inserting one of the center patterns—a child's name, initials, or monogram—by adjusting the size of the border and design to fit together. (You can do this on a copy machine at a copy shop.)

Daniel

Cameo Bear

10" x 12" made by the author

Materials

Fabric: ¾ yard

Wool batting to fit the cameo

Lace trim: 1¼ yards

Hanging hook: You can find white plastic-like rings at a craft store or metal washers at a hardware store.

Ribbon: 1 yard – If you use French ribbon with wire on the edges, you can manipulate a nice looking bow.

Cutting

Print a copy of the oval circle using paper heavy enough to trace around. Cut 2 ovals from the fabric.

Cut out a piece of batting the same size.

Binding: Cut 1¼" wide bias strips to equal a length of 36".

Making the Wallhanging

Mark the bear and border quilting designs.

Add trapunto, if you choose, or use wool batting.

Do not add lace trim. Because of the continuous curved edge, lace will not lie flat when turned to the outside, so a simple binding is all you need.

Sandwich the marked front, batting, and back. Add stabilizing stitches and quilt the design.

To check to see that the cameo shape has not been distorted by the quilting, fold the cameo horizontally (top to bottom) and make adjustments for any out-of-oval spots that might have developed. Trim off any little bulges, but be careful not to trim so much that you end up with a too-small cameo. Repeat, folding vertically (side-to-side).

Join the edges and add the binding.

If you put the binding on with a very small amount of stretch in it, you will notice that the center begins to form a slight bulge and this is exactly the look you want. It adds to the cameo effect.

Hand sew the binding to the back, working the slight bulge in with your hands.

Finishing Touches

To add a hanging loop, cut a piece of fabric 2" x 1½". Fold the piece lengthwise, right sides together, and stitch a ¼" seam on the long side. Turn right side out.

Insert this piece through a plastic loop and position the loop on the back so that it comes to the top edge of the cameo without showing on the front side. Fold under the open bottom edges of the loop and hand sew them, making sure the stitches don't show on the front.

Rinse or spritz out any wash-a-way thread and blue markings.

Encourage the rounded, curved, cameo look by shaping it with your hands before laying it out to dry.

Thread the ribbon through the hanging loop and tie a bow so that it falls over the top of the cameo toward the front.

ABC

3½" x 3½", made by the author

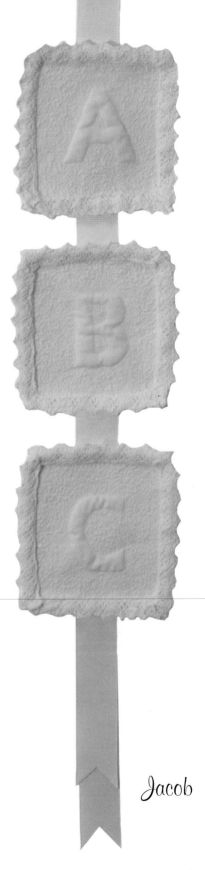

Materials

Fabric: ¼ yard

Wool batting: 3 squares 5" x 5"

Lace: 1⅓ yard. These little quilts are small, so a narrower lace trim is better.

Ribbon: 1 yard

Loop: I found a metal loop at the hardware store in the nuts, bolts, and washer section.

Cutting

You may make these ABC squares any size you like. With a 1" ribbon, I made squares 3"–4". If your ribbon is wider and your loop is larger, you can make larger squares. Adjust the letters (pages 42–44) to fit the size of your squares.

Cut 6 squares the same size.

If you want letters to spell out the child's name, you'll need 3 more squares for each additional letter.

Making the Wallhanging

Mark the quilting design.

Sew the lace to the front of the squares putting 3 little tucks at each corner—one before the corner, one at the corner, and one just beyond the corner.

Add trapunto, if you choose, or use wool batting.

Sandwich the layers for each square with the batting on the bottom, then the back right side up, and the front right side down. Carefully match and pin the 3 layers together all the way around.

Sew the layers together, beginning on the left side of the bottom edge of each of the ABC squares, stopping 2"–3" from where you started. Leave an opening on the bottom so the square can be turned right side out.

Pull the front and back apart, keeping the batting and the back together, and turn right side out through the opening at the bottom. Gently pull the lace out from the layers. Insert a chopstick or a crochet hook to gently push the corners out.

Working from the back side, turn under the open part at the bottom of the square. Pin it

in place and hand sew this small section together.

Put silk thread in the top of your machine and cotton thread in the bobbin. Using a walking foot, add topstitching ⅛" in from the edge.

This wallhanging is small, so you may not need to add stabilizing stitches. Quilt the design.

Rinse or spritz out any wash-a-way thread and blue markings. Let dry.

Finishing Touches

Cut a piece of ribbon about one yard long. Insert it through the metal loop and bring the ends together. Cut a V shape in both ends. Arrange the three ABC squares below the loop with a pleasing distance between them. Hand sew them in place on the back side so that the stitches do not show on the front.

Baby Girl's Bonnet

Materials

Fabric: ½ yard

Lace trim: ½ yard

Choose a lace that will not fall into the baby's face.

Buttons: 2 heirloom-style buttons.

Wool batting: one piece 6½" x 15½" and one piece 5½" x 6½"

Cutting

Cut 3 pieces of fabric 6½" x 15½" for the bonnet front (the top and sides).

Cut 3 pieces 5½" x 6½" for the bonnet back.

Cut 2 pieces 2" x 15" for the ties.

Making the Bonnet

Fold the bonnet pieces in half to mark the centers on the 15½" long and the 5½" long edges. Match the centers, right sides together, and sew each bonnet back to a front piece, making 3 separate T-shaped units as shown—an outside, a backing for the quilting, and a lining.

Mark the quilting design.

Sandwich the marked unit with the batting and an unmarked unit. Add stabilizing stitches and quilt the design.

Check all sides to make sure the straight edges have not been distorted by the quilting. Trim if necessary.

Position the lace along the top front edge of the bonnet with right sides together and the outside lace edge facing in toward the center of the bonnet. Sew with a ¼" seam. Do not stretch the lace as you sew it down. Leave the ends of the lace flat and trim them even with the bonnet. The lace will be sewn into the seams when the lining is added.

Fold the two 2" x 15" strips in half lengthwise, right sides together, and press. Sew across one end at a 45-degree angle and down the long edge with a scant ¼" inch seam.

Trim a scant ¼" away from the sewn 45-degree angle.

Turn right side out with the help of a chopstick or crochet hook, being careful not to puncture the sewn end. Press flat.

Sew each of the ties with a ¼" seam onto the front edges of the bonnet, on top of the lace and about ½" in from the bottom edge of the bonnet on either side. The open end of the ties will be facing toward the front of the bonnet.

Place the quilted unit and lining right sides together aligning the back edges where the smaller pieces were sewn. Pin together with the quilted unit on top.

The lining was cut the same size as the outside but will be bigger at this point, depending on how much quilting you have done.

Trim off the excess lining

Beginning at one edge of the bottom of the small back piece and continuing all the way around, sew the quilted unit and lining together with a ¼" seam, pivoting at the corners. Stop 2"–3" from where you started, leaving the back bottom section open.

Clip the corners at the intersection of the front and small back piece so they won't pucker when turned. Check that the ties did not get caught in one of the seams.

Turn right side out, using a chopstick to poke out the corners.

Put a stabilizing stitch in the ditch in the seam connecting the front and back pieces of the bonnet.

Turn in the open seam on the bottom of the small back piece about ¼". Press, pin, and stitch closed.

You will notice that the lace trim turns back where the ties have been sewn in. This is correct, and done this way so the lace will be away from baby's chin when the bonnet is tied at the neck.

Finishing Touches

Put button holes at the back bottom corners of the front piece.

Sew buttons onto the outside corners of the back piece, placing them about ½" in on each side.

Rinse or spritz out any wash-a-way thread and blue marking pen. Let dry.

Fasten the buttons to finish the bonnet.

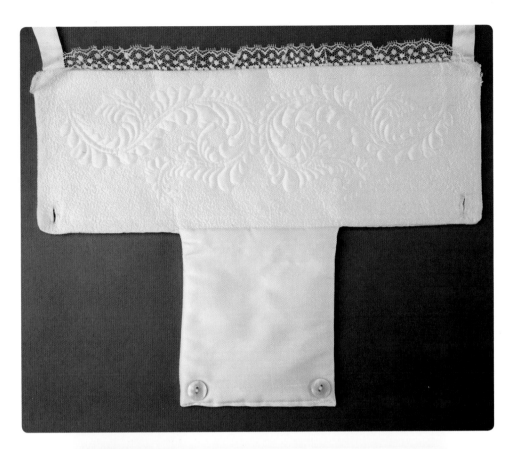

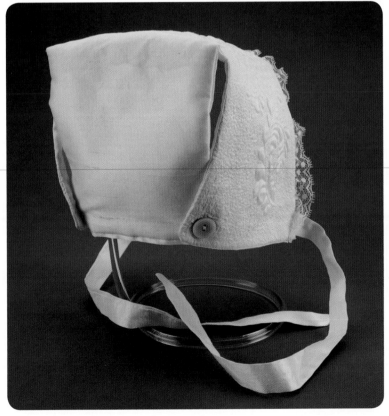

Quilts

Approximately 24" x 40", made by the author

Materials

Fabric: 2½ yards
Lace trim: 4½ yards
Wool batting: 31" x 44"

Cutting

Fold fabric selvage-to-selvage.

For the quilt top and backing, cut two sections 31" x width of the fabric.

For the binding, cut 4 strips 2¼" wide.

If you choose to add a hanging sleeve, cut one strip 8" wide.

Cut a piece of batting the same size as the quilt top fabric.

Making the Quilt

Print a copy of the quilting design of your choice. Mark the quilting design onto the quilt top fabric.

Add trapunto if you choose.

Sandwich the marked backing, batting, and top. Add stabilizing stitches and quilt the design.

The cutting measurements allow for extra fabric beyond the border designs. You may put grid lines or as much background quilting in this space as you like. If you need to trim off more when you square up your quilt, there is enough fabric to do that.

Square up the quilt.

Connect the edges and add the lace trim.

Apply the binding but do not hand finish yet. Fold the lace away from the quilt and topstitch through all layers.

For the hanging sleeve, cut the 8" strip to fit the width of the quilt. Fold over and sew a small finishing hem on both ends. Fold the sleeve in half lengthwise, wrong sides together, and press.

Pin the sleeve to the back of the quilt, aligning the raw edges with the edge of the quilt. Stitch with a scant ¼" seam.

Turn and hand finish the binding, enclosing the raw edges of the sleeve and covering the stitching line.

Rinse or spritz out any wash-a-way thread and blue markings. Let dry.

Allyson

Pillows

Sizes can vary; made by the author

Materials

Fabric: 1 yard
Lace trim: 1½ yards
Wool batting: 1 yard
Velcro® brand tape: 6" for each pillow
12" x 12", 14" x 14", or 12" x 16" pillow form

Cutting

The cutting sizes given below are larger than the amount needed for the pillow forms. You will be trimming them back when you square up the top.

For a 12" x 12" pillow, cut 2 pieces 15" x 15" for the front and 2 pieces 9" x 15" for the back.

For a 14" x 14" pillow, cut 2 pieces 17" x 17" for the front and 2 pieces 10" x 17" for the back.

For a 12" x 16" pillow, cut 2 pieces 15" x 19" for the front and 2 pieces 10" x 15" for the back.

Cut 2 strips 2¼" for the binding for all these pillow sizes.

Cut 1 piece of wool batting the same size as the front piece.

Making the Pillows

Mark the quilting design on the front of the pillow and sandwich it with the batting and backing. Add stabilizing stitching and quilt the design.

The edges will be cut off when you square the top, so keep that in mind when you are adding in background quilting.

Tamara

Stacie

Square up the project so that the top is ½" larger than the dimensions of your pillow form.

Connect the edges and add the lace trim.

To make the pillow back, press under ¼" of one long side of both back pieces, then fold over again with a 1" fold. Press. Stitch along the folded edge .

Center the hook portion of a 6" length of Velcro on one of the folds and stitch in place.

Center the loop portion on the outside of the opposite piece and stitch in place.

Overlap the two pieces, closing the Velcro opening.

Center the finished quilted front on top of the back, wrong sides together. The pillow top may have changed in size because of the quilting. Carefully trim off excess back fabric on all sides so that it is the same size as the top.

Pin together with the quilted side on top, and sew completely around the perimeter, following the same stitching line used to stitch on the lace.

Apply the binding but do not hand finish it yet.

Fold the lace away from the pillow and top-stitch through all layers.

Hand finish the binding.

Rinse or spritz out any wash-a-way thread and blue markings. Let dry.

Open the Velcro strips, insert the pillow form, and close.

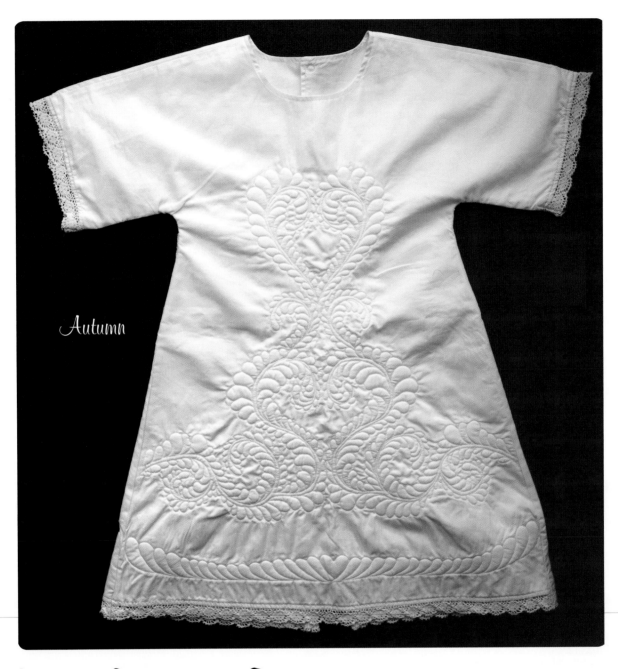

Autumn

Unisex Christening Gown

Infant size, made by the author

This is a gown worn for a special ceremony, or simply for photographs, by either a boy or girl baby. Think of it as a choir robe, or a minister's or priest's robe. It is worn over the baby's regular clothing or by itself, whichever way fits best.

Babies are christened at different ages and so weigh different amounts. It will fit a baby approximately 12 to 24 pounds; if the baby is 12 pounds it will drape down over the feet but if the baby is 24 pounds it might not reach the feet. Either fit is acceptable.

Materials

Fabric: 2 yards
Lace trim: 2 yards
Wool batting: ¼ yard
3 buttons: Choose flat, heirloom-looking buttons.

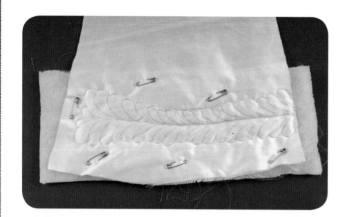

Cutting

Print a copy of the pattern using paper heavy enough to trace around.

Fold your fabric selvage-to-selvage. Place the center front of the pattern on the fold and place the center back just inside the selvage edge. Cut 2 front pieces and 4 back pieces—one set for the outside and one for the lining.

Cut a piece of batting using the front pattern piece. Cut 2 pieces of batting 6" x 14".

Making the Gown

The seam allowance is ¼" except where noted.

This gown is made with a lining. The batting is under the front and along the bottom quilting design of each back piece.

Mark the quilting design on the front and bottom edges of 2 back pieces.

Layer the wool batting with the front and the quilting areas at the bottom of the back pieces. Thread baste in place with wash-a-way thread.

Join the front and 2 back pieces at the shoulder, being sure to catch the front batting in the seams.

Join the front and 2 back pieces of the lining in the same way.

Sew lace to the bottom edge of the front, the 2 back pieces, and the sleeves ¼" from the edge of the fabric, with the outside lace edge facing into the center of the gown. The right side of the lace is facing the right side of the gown. Do not stretch the lace as you sew.

Trim the lace even with the edges of the gown so the lace will be caught in the seams when they are sewn.

Place the gown and the lining, right sides together, and pin all around the edges. Sew the 2 pieces together except for the lower edge of the sleeves.

Make 3 very small clips in the underarm seam.

Turn right side out by reaching in through the open end of a sleeve. Insert a chopstick to help get a good turn at the corners.

Lightly press the seams flat, pin, and add top stitching all around, ⅛" in from the edge, except on the side seams and underarms. The side seams will be joined after you finish the quilting.

Add stabilizing stitches and quilt the design.

Fold the sleeve lace out away from the gown. Fold under the lining, pin in place, and sew. Add top stitching ⅛" from the edge of the lace.

With right sides together, pin and sew the side seams, underarms, and sleeves with a ⅛" seam.

There are no cut edges to fray and this gives a finish to this seam similar to a French seam.

Make 3 buttonholes on one side of the back spaced 5" apart and sew buttons onto the other side of the gown.

Rinse or spritz out any wash-a-way thread and blue marking pen. Let dry.

Carroll

Quilting Patterns and Designs

Additional patterns for projects can be found on the accompanying CD.

Andrea

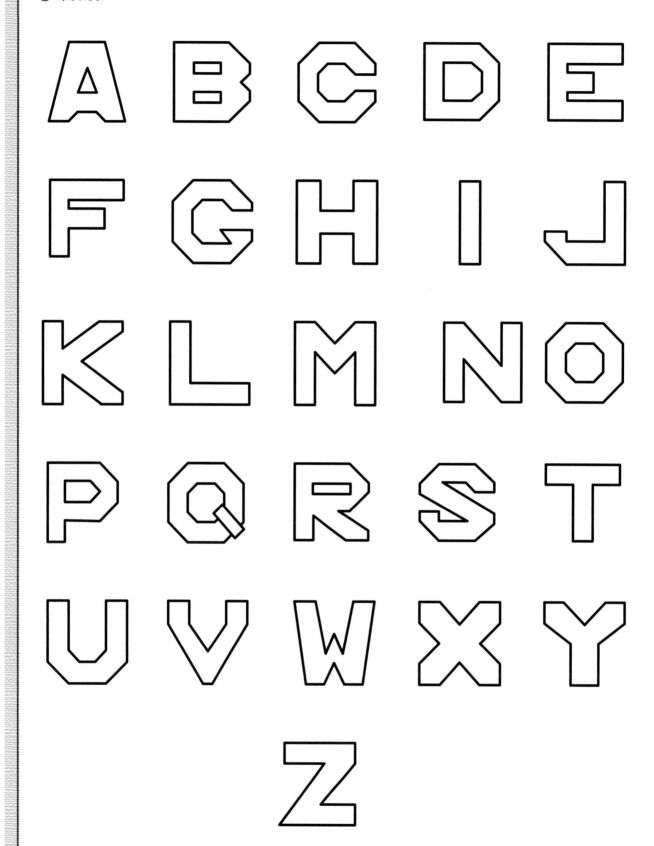

Alisa

A B C D E
F G H I J
K L M N O
P Q R S T
U V W X Y
Z

Lindsay

A B C D E

F G H I J

K L M N O

P Q R S T

U V W X Y

Z

Evan Border

Tatum Border

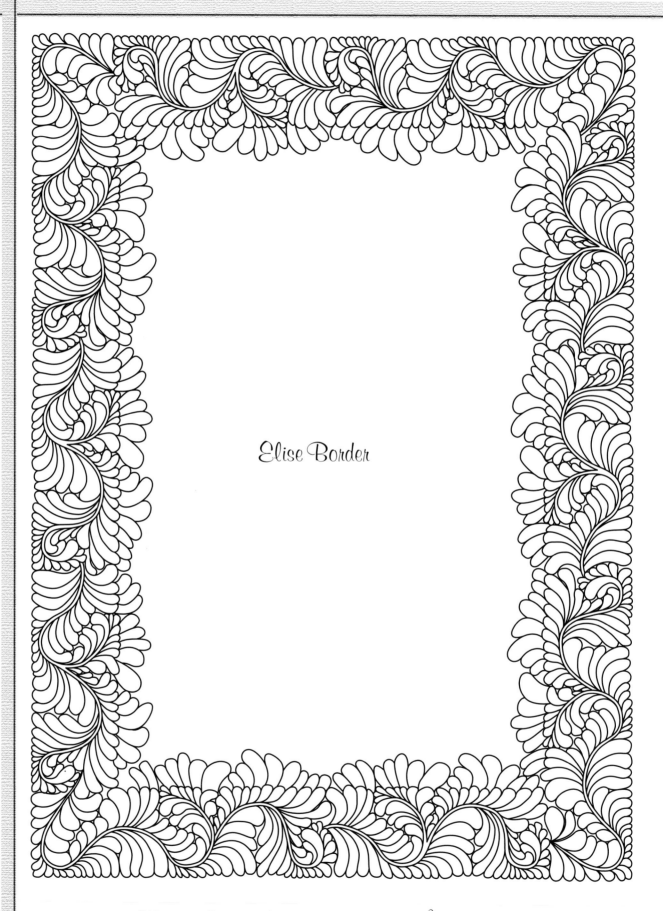

Elise Border

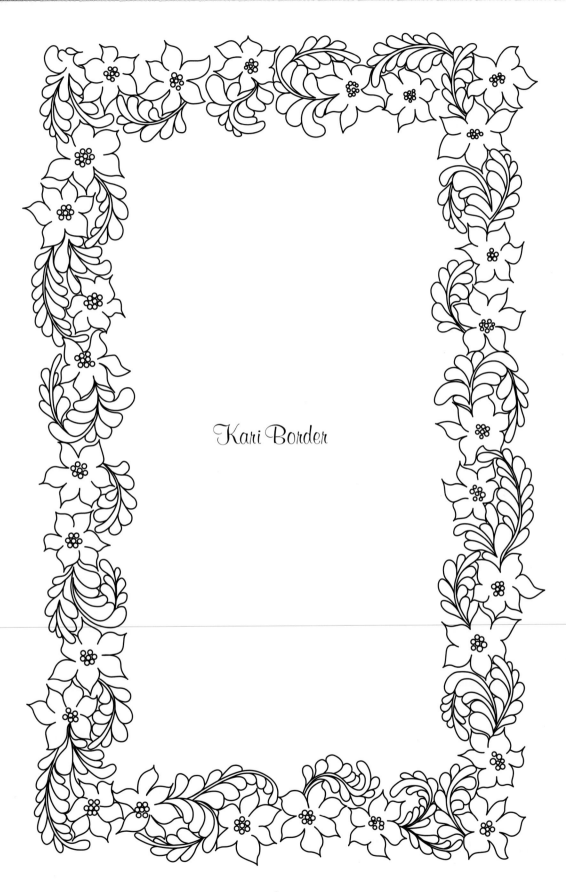

Kari Border

Sydney

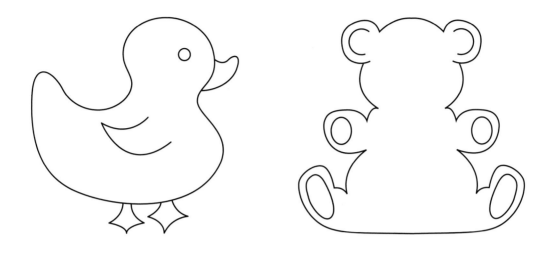

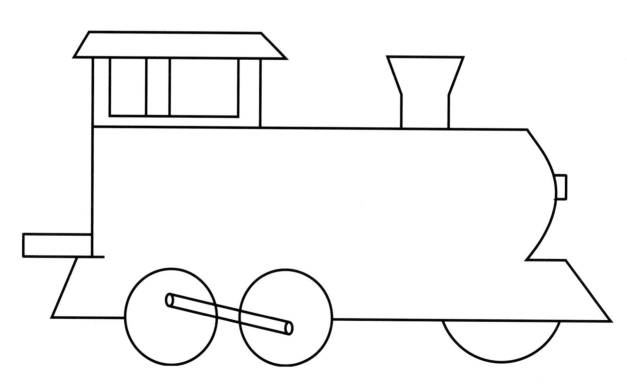

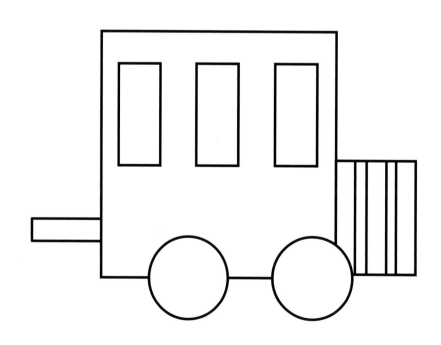

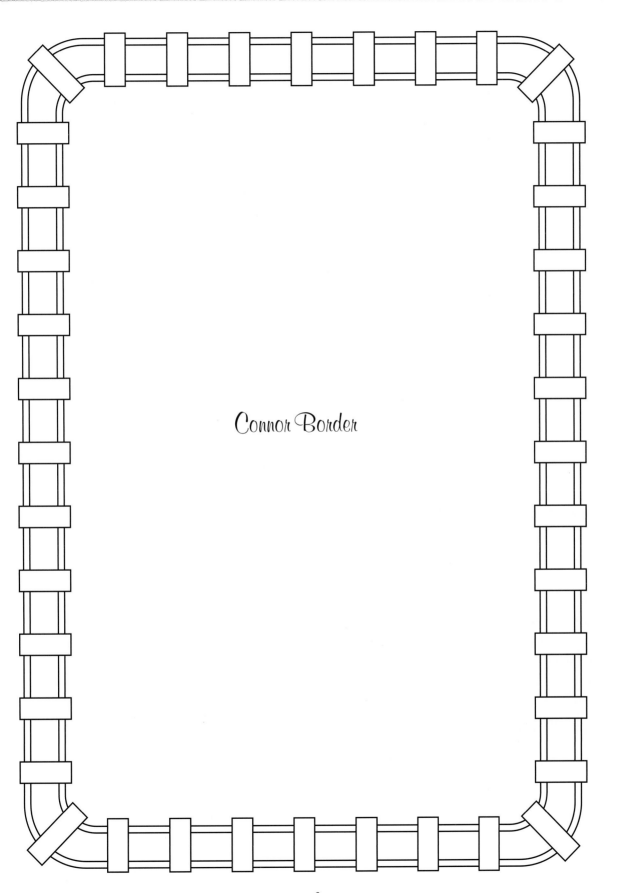

Connor Border

Resources

Artograph® Lightracer light box
2838 Vicksburg Lane North
Plymouth, MN 55447
Tel: 888-975-9555
Web site: www.artograph.com
This may also be purchased at Michaels®
stores.

Clover Water-Soluble Marker (thick)
Clover Needlecraft, Inc.
13438 Akibdra Blvd.
Cerritos, CA 90703
Tel: 800-233-1703
Web site: www.clover-USA.com

DMC® Thread
Ann Leatz
A to Z Designs (retail & wholesale)
402 Main Street
Dowagiac, MI 49047
Tel: 269-782-0635
Email: A2zDesign1@aol.com
Web site: www.AtoZdesigns.net

Hobbs Heirloom® Premium and Heirloom®
wool batting
Hancock's of Paducah
3841 Hinkleville Road
Paducah, KY 42001
Tel: 800-845-8723
Web site: www.hancocks-paducah.com

June Tailor® Grid Marker™ ruler
PO Box 208
2861 Highway 175
Richfield, WI 53076
Tel: 800-844-5400
Web site: www.junetailer.com

Silk and Wash-A-Way® thread
YLI Corporation
1439 Dave Lyle Blvd. #16-C
Rock Hill, SC 29730
Tel: 803-985-3100
Web site: www.ylicorp.com

VELCRO® is a registered trademark of Velcro
Industries B. V.

For dupioni shantung silk, Egyptian cotton,
lace trim, and buttons: Jo-Ann® Fabric and
Craft Stores or your local quilt shop

Books:

Dover books of alphabets and monograms
Dover Publications, Inc.
Web site: www.doverpublications.com

Diane Gaudynski
Guide to Machine Quilting and
Gaudynski's Machine Quilting Guidebook
Web site: www.dianegaudynski.net

Karen McTavish
Mastering the Art of McTavishing
Web site:www.designerquilts.com

About the Author

After graduating with a BS degree in zoology from Seattle Pacific University, I worked in medical laboratories and taught high school for a number of years.

From 1973 to 1981, my husband and I lived in Edinburgh, Scotland, while he studied at the University of Edinburgh. While there our son, Peter, was born, and for the next eighteen years I stayed at home and enjoyed being a mother. In Edinburgh I regularly participated in Embroiderers Guild meetings, but on returning to the United States I found there was very little interest in embroidery. Everyone was quilting.

Photo by Olan Mills

Even though I have sewn for as long as I can remember, I didn't take my first quilting class until about 1983. It was with Eleanor Burns on the Log Cabin block and I've never looked back. I have probably made at least seventy quilts and recently began entering quilts in shows. In 2007 I received a first place award in the Pieced Traditional Small category at the Glendale Quilt Show in Burbank, California, followed by a first-place award in the Medium Machine and Small Machine categories in 2008.

I have taught quilting to friends in my home but, because of work schedule and responsibilities, I have never taught formal classes. My husband was headmaster of a small private Christian high school in Los Angeles where I also worked. We endeavored to take students from low-income families and prepare them for university. We are now both retired and I am enjoying time for quilting. Our son, Peter, is with the U.S. Department of the Treasury in Washington, D.C.

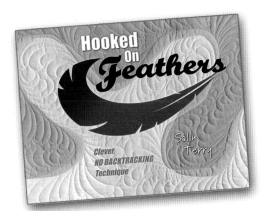

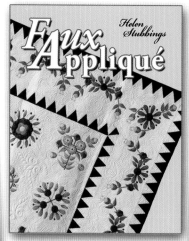

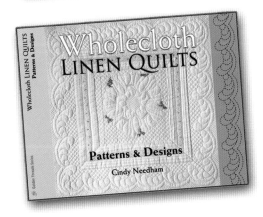
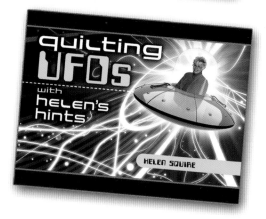